THE WORLD OF PLANTS

HOW DO PLANTS DEFEND THEMSELVES?

by Ruth Owen

PowerKiDS
press™

New York

Published in 2015 by The Rosen Publishing Group, Inc.
29 East 21st Street, New York, NY 10010

First Edition

Produced for Rosen by Ruby Tuesday Books Ltd
Editor for Ruby Tuesday Books Ltd: Mark J. Sachner
US Editor: Joshua Shadowens
Designer: Emma Randall

Publisher's Cataloging Data

Owen, Ruth.
How do plants defend themselves? / by Ruth Owen, first edition.
p. cm. — (The world of plants)
Includes index.
ISBN 978-1-4777-7157-0 (library binding) — ISBN 978-1-4777-7158-7 (pbk.) —
ISBN 978-1-4777-7159-4 (6-pack)
1. Plant defenses — Juvenile literature. 2. Plants, Protection of — Juvenile literature. I. Owen, Ruth, 1967–. II. Title.
QK921.O94 2015
580—d23

Manufactured in the United States of America

CPSIA Compliance Information: Batch #WS14PK8: For Further Information contact Rosen Publishing, New York, New York at 1-800-237-9932

Contents

Under Attack!

In the natural world, it's a daily battle for survival. Living things must grow, stay healthy, and **reproduce**. They must also avoid being eaten by other things. What do you do, though, if you're a plant and can't run from the many creatures that want to eat you?

To avoid becoming animal food, some **species** of plants have developed the **adaptation** of protective **spines**. Others have a defensive covering of vicious **thorns** on their stems.

Thorn

A rose with thorns on its stem

These beautiful angel's trumpets flowers are very poisonous.

Some plant species, however, have a means of defense that cannot be seen. These plants produce powerful **toxins** in their roots, stems, leaves, and flowers. The poisonous substances usually make the plant taste or smell bad. They can do serious

Spiny Cacti

If you are asked to think of a plant that's spiky, you'll probably think of a cactus. That's because when it comes to growing spines, these prickly plants are the masters.

Cacti grow in hot, dry **habitats**, such as **deserts**. Very little rain falls in deserts, so cacti have adapted to this lack of regular rain by storing water. When rain eventually does fall, cacti store as much water as possible in their thick, fleshy stems.

The only problem with this survival adaptation, however, is that it makes a cactus very attractive to desert animals. By eating a cactus's stems, an animal can obtain both food and water. Therefore, in order to defend against hungry, thirsty animals, cacti have sharp, protective spines.

Spines

A prickly pear's fleshy, spine-covered pads look like leaves but are actually the plant's stems.

Pad

Saguaro cactus spines

Arm

Main stem

A saguaro cactus's main stem and arms can store enormous quantities of water.

The fat, rounded stems of barrel cacti give these plants their name.

A barrel cactus's stems have ribs that expand and contract, like an accordion. When it rains, the plant takes in as much water as possible from the ground through its roots. Its ribs expand to allow the plant's sponge-like flesh to soak up gallons (l) of water. Once **hydrated**, the swollen stems of a barrel cactus may be over 90 percent water. In fact, during very dry times, a large plant can survive for more than five years by using its stored water.

With its juicy, water-soaked flesh, a barrel cactus is very **vulnerable** to thirsty desert animals. So the plant grows a dense covering of sharp, protective spines.

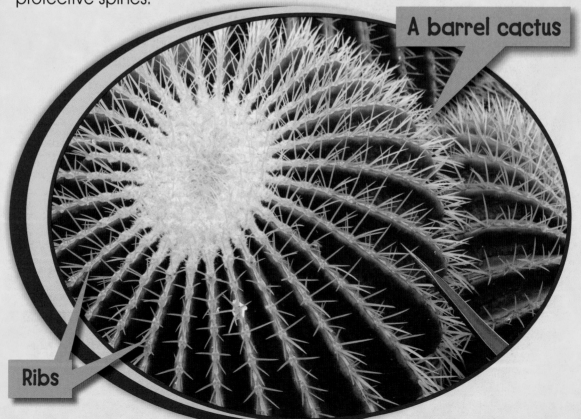

A barrel cactus

Ribs

Barrel cacti growing
in a desert

Dining on Spines

Cacti spines can inflict painful wounds. Some animals, however, are not put off by the plants' spiny armor.

Land iguanas are large lizards that live on the Galápagos Islands. In their hot, dry habitat, fresh water is scarce, so land iguanas feed on prickly pear cacti both as food and as a way to obtain water. Before eating, the lizards sometimes scrape large spines from the plants with their front feet. With their tough, leathery mouths, however, they are adapted to just munch into the cacti and eat the spines!

Some animals, such as rats, are small enough to move around between a cactus's spines. For these desert animals, cacti are an important source of food and water.

Dry prickly pear pad

Spiny Sunshades

The spines of cacti don't just defend the plants from animals. The hundreds or even thousands of spines on a cactus's stems protect the plant in another way, too.

Deserts are usually wide-open places. There are no large, leafy trees to create shade. Temperatures during the day in summer may reach 140 degrees Fahrenheit (60°C). Like any living thing, a plant can be damaged by the scorching heat of the Sun. Cacti, however, have their own personal sunshades.

A cactus spine might only be as thick as a needle, but it makes a thin, cooling shadow on the plant's stem. When there are thousands of spines, and each spine makes a shadow, it's enough to help shade a cactus from the desert sun.

Teddy bear cholla cacti get their name from their densely packed spines that look like fuzzy fur.

Shadows made by spines

Trees with Thorns

It's not just cacti that ward off hungry animals with spiky defensives. Some species of trees do, too.

Silk floss trees are truly beautiful plants that produce a mass of pink flowers in spring. Take a close-up look at the tree's trunk, though, and you'll see that it's covered with thousands of protective dagger-like thorns.

Thorny acacia trees grow on dry **grasslands** in Africa. With few plants around, and lots of hungry plant-eaters, these trees grow sharp thorns to protect their leaves from being eaten. Not every animal is put off by the trees' weaponry, however. Giraffes are able to twist and turn their 20-inch- (50-cm) long tongues between the thorns to grab the leaves.

Silk floss tree

Thorns on a silk floss tree's trunk

Acacia tree thorns

Thorns and Stinging Ants

Whistling acacia or whistling thorn trees are protected by thorns and by armies of ants that live in their branches.

The thorns of these trees have round, swollen bases. Ants make their homes in the bases of the thorns, and feed on a sweet liquid called **sap** that's produced by the trees' leaves. If another animal tries to eat the tree's leaves, the ants sting the intruder's mouth. The ants are protecting their food source, but at the same time they help protect the tree from being eaten.

Whistling thorn trees get their name because they make a whistling noise. The rounded bases of the thorns, where the ants live, have tiny entrance and exit holes. The whistling sound is made when wind blows over these holes.

Swollen, rounded base of thorn

Ants

The thorns of a whistling thorn tree

Everyday Defenses

Many everyday plants, such as roses and blackberry bushes, that grow in gardens and even on roadsides have impressive defenses.

Rose plants grow colorful, scented flowers that attract bees and other insects that **pollinate** the flowers so the plant can produce seeds. Blackberry bushes produce leaves, flowers, and seeds inside sweet berries. These plant parts taste good to many animals. As a means of defense, the stems of these plants produce thorns. Some thorns are large, hard, and woody. Other thorns grow as a mass of tiny, hairlike prickles.

A prickly defense doesn't always stop animals from eating a plant, however. Goats, deer, and many other plant-eaters will do battle with painful thorns to feed on new green **shoots**, tasty roses, or juicy blackberries.

Even the thinnest stems of this blackberry bush are smothered in tiny prickles.

This beautiful rose plant has stems covered in savage thorns!

Protecting with Poison

Hidden inside the roots, stems, leaves, flowers, and fruits of some plants are deadly toxins, or poisons, that protect the plants from being eaten.

Scientists don't know for sure how animals learn to avoid eating poisonous plants. The poisons may make the plants taste unpleasant.

These yellow flowers are poisonous buttercups.

Foxglove flower

Sometimes animals might eat a small amount of a plant, get sick, and then learn not to eat that plant again. Young animals watch their mothers and learn which plants the adults avoid eating. The knowledge of which plants are dangerous is then passed on from generation to generation.

Buttercups and foxgloves are two poisonous wild plants that often grow thickly in pastures where sheep, horses, and other grazing animals live. The animals will avoid these plants, however, eating every other plant around them.

Aconitums are flowering plants that grow in gardens and in the wild.

Every part of these pretty plants is poisonous. Eating just a tiny piece of an aconitum causes severe stomach pains and vomiting. The plant's poison also makes the heart slow down and even stop beating! People have even been poisoned by touching the plant and absorbing its poisons through their skin or through a wound.

These deadly plants are sometimes called wolfsbane. This name comes from ancient times when the plants were used to kill wolves that attacked sheep. Shepherds are said to have poisoned wolves by placing wolfsbane inside pieces of meat.

Aconitum is also known as monkshood because its flowers are shaped like the hood of a monk's cloak.

An aconitum plant

Deadly Berries

The berries of some plants look as if they would be good to eat—but are actually very dangerous!

Many plants grow berries as protective coverings for their seeds. To stop animals from eating the berries and destroying the seeds, however, the berries of some plants are highly poisonous. The berries of deadly nightshade and pokeweed plants can kill an animal or person.

Sometimes, however, berries that can kill most other animals don't harm birds. This is because plants need birds to spread their seeds to new growing places. A bird eats a berry, then the seeds pass unharmed through the animal's **digestive system**. Later, the seeds leave the bird's body in its waste and land on the ground, ready to start growing.

The glossy berries of the deadly nightshade plant are among the most dangerous berries in the world.

These pokeweed berries look delicious but are very toxic.

A mockingbird

Pokeweed berry

Don't Mess With Us!

There's one type of plant that almost everyone has touched at one time and then regretted it. The stinging nettle.

Growing on wasteland, at roadsides, and in wild places, these leafy plants don't look as if they have powerful defenses. Touch their leaves or stems, though, and hundreds of tiny hairs will inject a liquid into your skin that stings—a lot! Not all species of nettles are dangerous, but always be careful.

Tiny stinging hairs

Stinging nettles

26

Plants may not be able to run from people and other animals, but many plants are not defenseless. From stinging hairs to sharp spines, pointed thorns to powerful poisons, plants have developed very effective adaptations to defend themselves from becoming food for hungry animals.

INVESTIGATION 1:

Protection from the Sun

In this investigation, see how a cactus's spines create cooling shade on the plant's stems.

Step 1:

Use the craft knife to cut the sponge into the shape of a cactus. Stand the sponge cactus in the dish so it doesn't fall over.

(Only use a knife if an adult is there to help you.)

Step 2:

Push toothpicks into the sponge to create spines.

Step 3:

Place the sponge cactus in a sunny spot. Are the spines creating shadows?

Why? How? What?

How could your cactus receive more protection from the Sun?

(See page 32 for the answer.)

28

INVESTIGATION 2: Storing Water

A cactus needs protective spines because its ability to store water in its flesh makes it a target for hungry, thirsty animals. In this investigation, check out how a cactus absorbs water and also see how its waxy outer skin stops the water inside its stems from evaporating, or drying out.

You will need:
- Two small kitchen sponges
- A craft knife
- Two small dishes
- A measuring cup and water
- Wax paper

Step 1:

Use the craft knife to cut each sponge into the shape of a cactus. You can reuse your cactus from investigation 1. Make sure both sponge cacti are the same shape and size. **(Only use a knife if an adult is there to help you.)**

Step 2:

Stand each cactus in a dish and pour a cup of water into each dish. Wait for the cacti to soak up the water—just like the flesh of a cactus absorbing water.

Step 3:

Remove the cacti from their dishes. Now wrap one of the sponge cacti in wax paper. Leave the two cacti on a counter top to dry out.

Why? **How?** What?

Which sponge cactus dried out first?
Why do you think the cacti dried at different speeds?
(See page 32 for the answer.)

Glossary

adaptation (a-dap-TAY-shun) A physical change or change in behavior that happens over time and makes a plant or animal more able to survive in its environment.

deserts (DEH-zurts) Places that receive less than 10 inches (25 cm) of rain or snow each year. Deserts can be hot or cold. They are often sandy or rocky, with few trees and other plants.

digestive system (dy-JES-tiv SIS-tem) The group of body parts, including the stomach and intestines, that break down food so that a body can use it for fuel.

grasslands (GRAS-landz) Hot habitats with lots of grass and few trees or bushes. Sometimes it is very dry, and at other times there is lots of rain.

habitats (HA-buh-tats) Places where animals or plants normally live. A habitat may be a backyard, a forest, the ocean, or a mountainside.

hydrated (HY-dray-ted) Having absorbed water.

pollinate (PAH-luh-nayt) To move pollen from the anthers of one flower to the stigma of another.

reproduce (ree-pruh-DOOS) To make more of something, such as when plants make seeds that will grow into new plants.

sap (SAP) A liquid in the stems of plants that carries food and water throughout the plant.

shoots (SHOOTS) New parts of a plant, such as leaves, that emerge from underground or from a plant's stems.

species (SPEE-sheez) One type of living thing. The members of a species look alike and can reproduce together.

spines (SPYNZ) Thin, spiky parts that grow on the stems of cacti and protect the plants from being eaten by animals.

thorns (THORNZ) Pointed, hard, parts of a plant's stem that protect the plant from being eaten by animals.

toxins (TOK-sunz) Harmful, poisonous substances.

vulnerable (VUL-nuh-ruh-bul) Able to be harmed.

Websites

Due to the changing nature of Internet links, PowerKids Press has developed an online list of websites related to the subject of this book. This site is updated regularly. Please use this link to access the list:

www.powerkidslinks.com/wop/defend/

Read More

Green, Jen. *Life in the Desert*. New York: Gareth Stevens, 2010.

Miller, Connie Colwell. *The World's Deadliest Plants on Earth*. Mankato, MN: Capstone Press, 2010.

Smith, Lucy Sackett. *Giraffes: Towering Tall*. New York: PowerKids Press, 2010.

Index

Answers

INVESTIGATION 1:
One way for your sponge cactus to receive more protection is to add more spines. You can also try turning your cactus and watching how the shadows made by the spines change size and shape. Try to find a position for your cactus where as much of its stem as possible is covered with shade.

INVESTIGATION 2:
The cactus sponge wrapped in wax paper probably took longer to dry out. That's because the water inside that sponge did not evaporate as quickly as in the other sponge. The sponge's waxy protective covering helped retain water, just as a cactus's waxy skin helps it retain its stored water.